BREADS

Cook Books from Amish Kitchens

Phyllis Pellman Good • Rachel Thomas Pellman

Good Books

Intercourse, PA 17534
800/762-7171
www.goodbks.com

BREADS

Cook Books from Amish Kitchens

A warm, moist, pungent smell through the house. A steaming loaf of bread just lifted from the oven! Thoughts of cinna-

mon rolls, glazed dough-nuts, and corn pone will make any child hungry for home. For these foods are rich in flavor and affection and warm memories of big kitchens full of love.

Cover art and design by Cheryl A. Benner.
Design and art in body by Craig N. Heisey; calligraphy by Gayle Smoker.
This special edition is an adaptation of *Breads: From Amish and Mennonite Kitchens, Pennsylvania Dutch Cookbooks,* and from *Cook Books by Good Books.* Copyright © 1982, 1991, 1996 by Good Books, Intercourse, PA 17534. ISBN: 1-56148-196-3. All rights reserved. Printed in the United States of America.

Contents

White Bread

1 pkg. dry yeast

½ cup warm water

⅓ cup sugar

2 tsp. salt

2 cups warm water

2½ Tbsp. melted shortening

6-7 cups flour

Makes 2 loaves

1. Dissolve yeast in ½ cup warm water.
2. In large bowl combine sugar, salt, water, and shortening. Add yeast mixture. Gradually add flour to form a soft dough. Turn onto floured surface and knead until smooth. Place in greased bowl. Cover and let rise about 2 hours. Punch down. Divide into 2 portions and form loaves. Place in greased bread pans. Prick tops with fork. Let rise until higher than pans (about 2 hours).
3. Bake at 375° for 25-30 minutes. Cool 10 minutes. Butter tops of loaves. Place pans on sides until loosened. Remove bread and cool completely.

Whole Wheat Bread

2 pkgs dry yeast   Makes 4 loaves
4 cups warm water
½ cup soft margarine or butter
¼ cup molasses
½ cup honey
2 tsp. salt
6 cups whole wheat flour
4 cups white flour

1. Dissolve yeast in warm water.
2. Combine margarine, molasses, honey, and salt. Mix well. Add yeast mixture. Gradually add flour. Turn onto floured surface and knead until smooth. Place in greased bowl and let rise until double. Punch down. Let dough rest a few minutes. Shape into 4 loaves. Place in greased bread pans. Let rise about 1 hour. Bake at 375° for 35-40 minutes.

Said the tester, "This is the best loaf of brown bread I ever made!"

Potato Bread

3½ cups milk   Makes 3 loaves
6 Tbsp. sugar
6 Tbsp. butter
2 tsp. salt
½ cup mashed potatoes
2 pkgs. dry yeast
½ cup lukewarm water
3 cups whole wheat flour
7-8 cups white flour

1. Scald milk. Add sugar, butter, salt, and mashed potatoes. Cool to lukewarm.
2. Meanwhile, dissolve yeast in water. Add to cooled milk mixture.
3. Add whole wheat flour and 1 cup white flour. Beat 2 minutes with mixer. Stir in 6-7 more cups flour until dough leaves sides of bowl.
4. Turn onto lightly floured surface. Knead lightly till dough forms a smooth ball. Place in greased bowl. Turn once to grease top of dough. Cover and let rise in a warm place away from drafts until doubled, 1½ - 2 hours. Punch down and let rise again till double. Turn onto floured surface and divide dough into 3 equal parts. Cover

and let rest 10 minutes.

5. Form 3 loaves and place in greased bread pans which have been sprinkled with cornmeal (about 1 Tbsp. per pan.)

6. Bake at 350° for 40-45 minutes. Remove from pans and place on rack to cool.

Steamed Bread Dumplings

Make your favorite white bread dough. When ready to be baked, take part of the dough and form bun size balls. Place in a buttered baking dish (about 2" deep) and steam over boiling water for 30 minutes. Serve hot with fruit and milk.

"These can be served also as dessert with sliced canned peaches and milk."

Oatmeal Bread

1 pkg. dry yeast   Makes 2 loaves
½ cup warm water
1 cup quick oats
½ cup whole wheat flour
½ brown sugar or molasses
1 Tbsp. salt
2 Tbsp. margarine
2 cups boiling water
5-6 cups flour

1. Dissolve yeast in warm water.
2. In large bowl combine oats, whole wheat flour, sugar, salt, and margarine. Pour boiling water over all and mix well. When mixture is cooled to lukewarm stir in yeast.
3. Stir in approximately half of flour. Turn onto floured surface and knead in remaining flour.
4. Place in greased bowl. Cover and let rise until double. Punch down. Shape into two loaves and place in greased bread pans. Let rise again. Bake at 350° for 30-40 minutes. Cool on rack, brushing loaves with margarine for a soft crust.

Rye Bread

Makes 3 loaves

1 pkg. dry yeast
½ cup warm water
2 cups rye flour
¾ cup dark molasses
⅓ cup shortening
2 tsp. salt
2 cups boiling water
6-6½ cups white flour

1. Dissolve yeast in warm water.
2. In large bowl, combine rye flour, molasses, shortening, salt, and boiling water. Mix well. Cool to lukewarm. Add yeast mixture. Gradually add white flour to make a soft dough. Turn onto floured surface and knead well.
3. Place dough in greased bowl. Turn once to grease surface. Cover and let rise until double (about 1½-2 hours). Punch down in bowl. Cover and let rise again until double (about 30 minutes). Turn onto floured surface. Shape into 3 loaves and place in well greased bread pans. Let rise again (about 30 minutes). Bake at 350° for 35-40 minutes. Remove from pans. Cover loaves with dish towel and cool on racks.

Ada's Dill Bread

Makes 3 loaves

2 pkgs. dry yeast
1 cup warm water
2 cups warmed cottage cheese
4 Tbsp. sugar
2 Tbsp. minced onion
3 tsp. dill weed
2 tsp. salt
½ tsp. baking soda
2 eggs
1 Tbsp. oil
5½ - 6½ cups flour

1. Dissolve yeast in warm water.
2. Combine all ingredients except flour and beat well. Add flour gradually. Turn onto floured surface and knead until smooth.
3. Place in greased bowl and let rise until double. Punch down. Divide dough into 3 portions and form loaves. Put into 3 greased bread pans and let rise again.
4. Bake at 350° for 30 minutes. Lay foil over top of loaves to prevent over-browning and bake 15 minutes longer.

Raisin Bread

1 15 oz. box raisins   Makes 5 loaves
2 Tbsp. dry yeast
1 cup warm water
2 cups warm milk
½ cup oil
½ cup sugar
1 Tbsp. cinnamon
1 Tbsp. salt
2 eggs, beaten
8-10 cups flour

1. Soak raisins 3-4 hours or overnight. Drain.
2. Dissolve yeast in warm water.
3. Combine milk, oil, sugar, cinnamon, salt, and eggs. Beat well. Add yeast and raisins.
4. Gradually add flour, stirring by hand. When dough becomes too stiff to stir, finish working in flour with hands.
5. Place dough in greased bowl. Cover and let rise in warm place about 1 hour. Punch down, knead and let rise another hour. Divide dough into 5 portions and form loaves. Place in greased pans and let rise another hour.
6. Bake at 300° for 50-60 minutes.

Sweet Rolls

1 pkg. dry yeast	Makes 2 dozen
¼ cup warm water	
¼ cup shortening	
¼ cup sugar	
1 cup milk, scalded, or 1 cup water	
1 tsp. salt	
1 egg, beaten	
3¼ - 4 cups flour	

1. Dissolve yeast in warm water.
2. In large bowl, combine shortening and sugar. Pour hot milk or water over mixture. Cool to lukewarm. Add 1 cup flour and beat well. Beat in yeast mixture and egg.
3. Gradually add remaining flour to form soft dough, beating well.
4. Brush top of dough with softened shortening. Cover and let rise in warm place until double (1½ - 2 hours). Punch down and knead. Form rolls. Let rise again until doubled. Bake according to variation instructions below.

Variations:
1. Divide dough in half. Roll each half into a rectangle approximately 12"x 8". Spread with butter and sprinkle with a

mixture of ½ cup brown sugar and 1 tsp. cinnamon. Roll as a jelly roll. Cut into 1-1½" slices. Place rolls in greased pans about ¾" apart. Let rise and bake at 350° for 30 minutes. Cool and spread with confectioner's sugar icing.

2. For pecan rolls, place ½ cup pecans in bottom of each of two greased 9½ x 5 x 3 inch pans. Make syrup by heating slowly: ½ cup brown sugar, ¼ cup butter, and 1 Tbsp. light corn syrup. Divide this syrup in half and pour half over each pan of pecans. Make rolls as in variation #1, cutting sugar to ¼ cup, and place on top of pecans and syrup. Let rise till double and bake at 375° for about 25 minutes. Remove from oven and turn pan upside down onto a flat plate. Syrup will run down through the rolls and pecans will be on top.

3. Make rolls as in variation #1, but sprinkle with raisins before rolling up. Bake as in #1.

Orange Rolls

1 cup shortening
⅔ cup sugar
1 Tbsp. salt
2 cups milk, scalded
3 Tbsp. dry yeast
1 cup warm water
½ cup orange juice
4 Tbsp. grated orange rind
4 eggs, beaten
11-13 cups flour

1. In large bowl, combine shortening, sugar, and salt. Scald milk and pour over shortening mixture.
2. Dissolve yeast in warm water.
3. When milk mixture is cooled, add orange juice, rind, eggs, and yeast. Mix well.
4. Gradually add flour, mixing with spoon. After adding about 8 cups, place on floured surface and knead in remaining flour.
5. Place in greased bowl and let rise till double. Roll about ¾" thick and cut with biscuit cutter. Place in greased baking pans about 1 inch apart. Let rise until double.
6. Bake at 325° for 20-25 minutes.
7. When cooled ice with Orange Icing.

Orange Icing

  4 Tbsp. orange juice
  1 Tbsp. grated orange peel
  3 cups 10x sugar

Combine and mix until smooth.

Cinnamon Flop

  1 cup sugar   Makes 2 9"pans
  2 cups flour
  2 tsp. baking powder
  1 Tbsp. melted butter
  1 cup milk
  brown sugar, cinnamon, and butter for top

1. Sift sugar, flour, and baking powder together.
2. Add butter and milk and stir until well blended.
3. Divide mixture between 2 9" pie or cake pans, well greased.
4. Sprinkle tops with flour, then brown sugar, then cinnamon. Push chunks of butter into the dough. This makes holes and later gets gooey as it bakes. Bake at 350° for 30 minutes.

Cinnamon Rolls

Makes 4 dozen

½ cup sugar
½ cup shortening
1½ tsp. salt
1 cup milk, scalded
1 cup lukewarm water
2 pkgs. dry yeast
2 eggs, beaten
½ tsp. nutmeg (optional)
7 cups flour

Filling

6 Tbsp. melted butter
1½ cups brown sugar
1 Tbsp. cinnamon
1 cup raisins (optional)

1. In large bowl, combine sugar, shortening, and salt. Scald milk and pour over shortening mixture.
2. Combine yeast and warm water and set aside to dissolve.
3. When milk mixture has cooled, add beaten eggs, dissolved yeast, and nutmeg. Beat well.
4. Gradually add flour, beating well. Turn onto floured surface and knead lightly,

adding only enough flour so dough can be handled. Place in greased bowl. Cover and let rise in warm place until double (about 2 hours).

5. Divide dough in half. Roll each piece into rectangles. about ¼" thick. Brush with melted butter and sprinkle with mixture of brown sugar and cinnamon. Sprinkle with raisins. Roll up like jelly roll and cut slices ½" thick.

6. Place slices 1" apart in greased baking pans. Let rise about 1 hour.

7. Bake at 375° for 20 minutes.

"These always bring ooh's and aah's from guests!"

Sara King's Doughnuts

¾ cup lard or shortening   Makes 2½ dozen
¾ cup sugar
1 cup hot water
1 cup warm water
2 pkgs. dry yeast
2 eggs, beaten
1 tsp. salt
6 or more cups flour

1. In large bowl combine shortening, sugar, and warm water.
2. Add yeast to water and set aside to dissolve.
3. When shortening mixture has cooled, add eggs, salt, yeast mixture, and flour.
4. Turn dough onto floured surface and knead until smooth and elastic. Cover and set in warm place. Let rise until double. Roll dough about ½" thick and cut with drinking glass or doughnut cutter without the hole. Let rise again until double.
5. Fry doughnuts in deep fat until browned, turning once. Cool and fill. To fill, cut a small hole with a sharp knife. Force filling into doughnut with a cookie press or cake decorator.

Filling

    4 cups 10x sugar
    1½ cups shortening
    2 egg whites
    2 Tbsp. flour
    2 tsp. vanilla
    4 Tbsp. milk

Combine all ingredients and beat until smooth.

Quick Waffles

Makes 10-12 waffles

    4 eggs
    2½ cups milk
    ¾ cup melted shortening
    3½ cups flour
    6 tsp. baking powder
    1 tsp. salt

1. Combine all ingredients and beat for 1 minute.
2. Bake waffles in hot waffle iron.

Glazed Potato Doughnuts

1 pkg. dry yeast   Makes 3½ dozen
¼ cup warm water
¼ cup shortening
¼ cup sugar
½ tsp. salt
1 cup scalded milk
¾ cup mashed potatoes
2 eggs, beaten
4-6 cups flour

1. Dissolve yeast in warm water.
2. Combine shortening, sugar, salt, and milk. Cool to lukewarm. Add yeast mixture, potatoes, and eggs. Beat well. Gradually add flour to make a soft dough. Turn onto floured surface and knead well. Place in a greased bowl. Cover and let rise until double (1-1½ hours). Punch down and let rest 10 minutes. Roll dough ½ inch thick. Cut with doughnut cutter. Let rise until double. Deep fry in hot oil (375°). Glaze or sprinkle with powdered or granulated sugar.

Glaze

- 1½ lb. confectioner's sugar
- 1½ Tbsp. melted butter
- 1½ tsp. vanilla
- warm milk (enough to make a soupy consistency)

Dip doughnuts in glaze. Allow excess glaze to drip off.

A drinking glass and a baby bottle may be used as a doughnut cutter. The top of the bottle makes the hole.

A word from the tester: "My two neighbor ladies helped me and responded by eating _most_ of them!"

Potato Doughnuts

1 cup mashed potatoes   Makes 2½ dozen
1½ Tbsp. melted shortening
2 eggs
½ cup milk
¼ cup sugar
½ tsp. salt
⅛ tsp. nutmeg
1 Tbsp. baking powder
2½ cups flour

1. Combine mashed potatoes and shortening. Add eggs and milk and beat well.
2. Gradually add dry ingredients and spices, mixing well.
3. Roll dough ¼-½ inch thick. Cut with doughnut cutter and fry in hot fat until nicely browned.

"When it's cold outside, serve these by the fireplace with tea."

Date and Nut Loaf

1 cup chopped dates   Makes 1 loaf
1 cup boiling water
1 tsp. soda
1 cup sugar
1 Tbsp. butter
1 egg
1 cup walnuts
1½ cups flour
1 tsp. vanilla

1. Sprinkle dates with soda and pour boiling water over all. Set aside.
2. Cream sugar, butter, and egg. Gradually stir in walnuts, flour, and vanilla. Combine with date mixture.
3. Pour into ungreased, paper-lined loaf pan or 8½ × 11 inch pan. Bake at 350° for 40-45 minutes.

"We usually serve this in the late afternoon at Christmas family gatherings."

Pumpkin Bread

3 cups sugar
1 cup oil
4 eggs
1 tsp. nutmeg
1 tsp. cinnamon
1½ tsp. salt
2 cups pumpkin, cooked and mashed
⅔ cup water
1 tsp. soda
½ tsp. baking powder
3 cups flour

1. Combine sugar, oil, eggs, nutmeg, cinnamon, and salt. Beat well.
2. Add remaining ingredients and mix well.
3. Pour batter into 2 loaf pans or 3 1-lb. coffee cans, which have been well greased. Bake at 350° for 1 hour. Slide bread out of pans or cans and cool.

Variations:
1. Add 1 cup chopped pecans to batter.
2. Add ⅔ cup raisins to batter.

Homemade Zucchini Bread

3 eggs   Makes 2 loaves
2 cups sugar
2 cups zucchini, shredded
1 cup cooking oil
2 tsp. vanilla
3 cups flour
1 tsp. salt
1 tsp. soda
1 tsp. baking powder
2 tsp. cinnamon
½ tsp. nutmeg
¼ tsp. cloves
½ cup chopped nuts
½ cup raisins (optional)

1. Beat eggs till foamy. Stir in sugar, zucchini, oil, and vanilla.
2. Gradually add dry ingredients and spices. Stir in nuts.
3. Pour into bread pans which have been greased only on the bottoms. Bake at 325° for 60-80 minutes. Cool 10 minutes. Remove from pans and cool completely. May be used as bread or frosted and served as cake.

Old Fashioned Walnut Bread

3 cups sifted flour   Makes 1 loaf
1 cup sugar
4 tsp. baking powder
1½ tsp. salt
1 egg, lightly beaten
¼ cup shortening, melted
1½ cups milk
1 tsp. vanilla
1½ cups walnuts, coarsely chopped

1. Sift together flour, sugar, baking powder, and salt.
2. Combine egg, shortening, milk, and vanilla and add to dry mixture. Stir just until all flour is moistened. Stir in walnuts.
3. Turn into a greased loaf pan or divide between 2 greased 2½ lb. cans. Bake at 350° for 80 minutes for loaf pan or about 70 minutes for cans.

Variation:
1. Blend ⅓ cup brown sugar, 1½ Tbsp. flour, 1 tsp. cinnamon, and 2 Tbsp. butter together. Prepare batter as directed. Pour half into loaf pan. Sprinkle streusel mixture

over batter. Top with remaining batter. Bake according to instructions.

2. Add 2 tsp. grated orange peel to egg and milk mixture. Add ¾ cup chopped candied fruit with the walnuts.

Green Tomato Bread

Makes 2 loaves

3 eggs
1½ cups sugar
1 cup vegetable oil
1 tsp. salt
1 Tbsp. vanilla
2 cups grated, drained, green tomatoes
3 cups flour
1¼ tsp. soda
½ tsp. baking powder
¾ cup raisins
1 cup chopped nuts

1. Beat eggs well. Add sugar, oil, salt, vanilla, and tomatoes.
2. Sift dry ingredients together. Gradually add to tomato mixture. Stir in raisins and nuts.
3. Pour into greased bread pans and bake at 350° for 45 minutes.

Corn Pone

1 cup sugar   Fills 1 9"x 13" pan
½ cup butter or shortening
2 eggs
1½ cups cornmeal
1½ cups flour
3 tsp. baking powder
½ tsp. salt
1½ cups milk

1. Cream sugar and shortening. Add eggs and beat well.
2. Combine cornmeal, flour, baking powder, and salt. Add alternately with milk.
3. Pour into a greased and floured 9"x 13" cake pan. Bake at 450° for 30-35 minutes.

Corn Meal Cakes

½ cup flour   Makes about 20 cakes
1½ cups yellow corn meal
2 tsp. baking powder
1 Tbsp. sugar
1 tsp. salt
1½ cups milk
1 Tbsp. liquid shortening

1. Combine all ingredients. Mix well.
2. Fry on greased griddle or skillet until browned.

Corn Meal Mush

1 qt. boiling water   Makes 2½ quarts
1 qt. cold water
2 cups yellow corn meal
½ cup white flour
1 tsp. salt

1. Put 1 qt. cold water in a heavy 4 qt. sauce-pan. Combine corn meal, flour, and salt and stir into cold water.
2. Slowly add boiling water, stirring constantly to prevent lumps.
3. Cover and cook slowly 1-3 hours just so mixture glops slowly.
4. Serve hot with cherry pie filling or thickened sour cherries and milk.

Note:
   Pour remaining mush in bread pan. Next day, slice and fry in oil for breakfast. Serve with molasses or syrup.

Apple Fritters

Makes 12 fritters

1 cup flour
1½ tsp. baking powder
½ tsp. salt
2 Tbsp. sugar
1 egg, beaten
½ cup plus 1 Tbsp. milk
1½ cups apples, pared and diced

1. Sift dry ingredients together. Beat egg and add milk. Pour into dry ingredients and stir until batter is smooth.
2. Pare and dice apples. Add apples to batter and blend well.
3. Drop by spoonfuls and fry in hot fat in heavy skillet. Fry until golden brown on both sides.

Variation:

Apples may be cored and sliced in round rings. Dip in batter and fry until golden brown.

Soda Biscuits

2 cups flour   Makes 12 biscuits
1 scant tsp. soda
1 scant tsp. cream of tartar
pinch of salt
3 Tbsp. shortening
1 cup sour milk or buttermilk

1. Rub dry ingredients and shortening together to make fine crumbs.
2. Add milk, stirring with fork until soft dough is formed.
3. Roll ½ inch thick and cut with biscuit cutter.
4. Bake at 450° for 10-12 minutes or until lightly browned.

Serve warm with butter and molasses or with gravy.

"My mother used this recipe a lot."

Bran Muffins

1 cup bran	Makes 12 muffins

½ cup whole wheat flour
½ cup wheat germ
½ cup sunflower seeds (optional)
1 cup raisins
3 tsp. baking powder
1 egg, well beaten
1 cup milk
⅓ cup oil
2 Tbsp. molasses
1 tsp. vanilla

1. Combine all dry ingredients. In separate bowl, combine all wet ingredients.
2. Pour wet ingredients over dry ingredients, mixing only till moistened.
3. Fill muffin pan about ¾ full. Bake at 350° for 20 minutes.

"They're healthy – and the kids love them!"